Gillespie

by Iain Gray

PUBLISHING

WRITING *to* REMEMBER

79 Main Street, Newtongrange,
Midlothian EH22 4NA
Tel: 0131 344 0414
E-mail: info@lang-syne.co.uk
www.langsyneshop.co.uk

Design by Dorothy Meikle
Printed by Blissetts
© Lang Syne Publishers Ltd 2024

All rights reserved. No part of this publication may be reproduced, stored or introduced into a retrieval system, or transmitted in any form or by any means (electronic, mechanical, photocopying, recording or otherwise) without the prior written permission of Lang Syne Publishers Ltd.

ISBN 978-1-85217-758-4

Gillespie

MOTTO:
Touch not the cat but (without) a glove
(Macpherson)

CREST:
A wildcat

TERRITORIES:
Lochaber, Strathspey

NAME variations include:
- Gilaspy
- Gilaspie
- Gilespie
- Gilespy
- Gillaspey
- Gillaspie
- Gillespay
- Gillespee

Chapter one:

The origins of the clan system

by Rennie McOwan

The original Scottish clans of the Highlands and the great families of the Lowlands and Borders were gatherings of families, relatives, allies and neighbours for mutual protection against rivals or invaders.

Scotland experienced invasion from the Vikings, the Romans and English armies from the south. The Norman invasion of what is now England also had an influence on land-holding in Scotland. Some of these invaders stayed on and in time became 'Scottish'.

The word clan derives from the Gaelic language term 'clann', meaning children, and it was first used many centuries ago as communities were formed around tribal lands in glens and mountain fastnesses.

The format of clans changed over the centuries, but at its best the chief and his family held the land on behalf of all, like trustees, and the ordinary clansmen and women believed they had a blood relationship with the founder of their clan.

There were two way duties and obligations. An inadequate chief could be deposed and replaced by someone of greater ability.

Clan people had an immense pride in race. Their relationship with the chief was like adult children to a father and they had a real dignity.

The concept of clanship is very old and a more feudal notion of authority gradually crept in.

Pictland, for instance, was divided into seven principalities ruled by feudal leaders who were the strongest and most charismatic leaders of their particular groups.

By the sixth century the 'British' kingdoms of Strathclyde, Lothian and Celtic Dalriada (Argyll) had emerged and Scotland, as one nation, began to take shape in the time of King Kenneth MacAlpin.

Some chiefs claimed descent from ancient kings which may not have been accurate in every case.

By the twelfth and thirteenth centuries the clans and families were more strongly brought under the central control of Scottish monarchs.

Lands were awarded and administered more and more under royal favour, yet the power of the area clan chiefs was still very great.

The long wars to ensure Scotland's

independence against the expansionist ideas of English monarchs extended the influence of some clans and reduced the lands of others.

Those who supported Scotland's greatest king, Robert the Bruce, were awarded the territories of the families who had opposed his claim to the Scottish throne.

In the Scottish Borders country – the notorious Debatable Lands – the great families built up a ferocious reputation for providing warlike men accustomed to raiding into England and occasionally fighting one another.

Chiefs had the power to dispense justice and to confiscate lands and clan warfare produced a society where martial virtues – courage, hardiness, tenacity – were greatly admired.

Gradually the relationship between the clans and the Crown became strained as Scottish monarchs became more orientated to life in the Lowlands and, on occasion, towards England.

The Highland clans spoke a different language, Gaelic, whereas the language of Lowland Scotland and the court was Scots and in more modern times, English.

Highlanders dressed differently, had different

customs, and their wild mountain land sometimes seemed almost foreign to people living in the Lowlands.

It must be emphasised that Gaelic culture was very rich and story-telling, poetry, piping, the clarsach (harp) and other music all flourished and were greatly respected.

Highland culture was different from other parts of Scotland but it was not inferior or less sophisticated.

Central Government, whether in London or Edinburgh, sometimes saw the Gaelic clans as a challenge to their authority and some sent expeditions into the Highlands and west to crush the power of the Lords of the Isles.

Nevertheless, when the eighteenth century Jacobite Risings came along the cause of the Stuarts was mainly supported by Highland clans.

The word Jacobite comes from the Latin for James – Jacobus. The Jacobites wanted to restore the exiled Stuarts to the throne of Britain.

The monarchies of Scotland and England became one in 1603 when King James VI of Scotland (1st of England) gained the English throne after Queen Elizabeth died.

The Union of Parliaments of Scotland and England, the Treaty of Union, took place in 1707.

Some Highland clans, of course, and Lowland families opposed the Jacobites and supported the incoming Hanoverians.

After the Jacobite cause finally went down at Culloden in 1746 a kind of ethnic cleansing took place. The power of the chiefs was curtailed. Tartan and the pipes were banned in law.

Many emigrated, some because they wanted to, some because they were evicted by force. In addition, many Highlanders left for the cities of the south to seek work.

Many of the clan lands became home to sheep and deer shooting estates.

But the warlike traditions of the clans and the great Lowland and Border families lived on, with their descendants fighting bravely for freedom in two world wars.

Remember the men from whence you came, says the Gaelic proverb, and to that could be added the role of many heroic women.

The spirit of the clan, of having roots, whether Highland or Lowland, means much to thousands of people.

Meanwhile, many families proudly boast the heraldic device known as a Coat of Arms, as featured on our front cover.

The central motif of the Coat of Arms would originally have been what was sometimes borne on the shield of a warrior to distinguish himself from others on the battlefield.

Not featured on the Coat of Arms, but highlighted on page three, is the family motto and related crest – with the latter frequently different from the central motif.

Clan warfare produced a society where courage and tenacity were greatly admired

Chapter two:

Battles of the clans

Both a given name and a surname, 'Gillespie' is of ecclesiastical roots, deriving as it does in Anglicised form from the Scottish-Gaelic *Mac Gille Easbuig* and also the Irish-Gaelic *Mac Giolla Easpaig*, denoting 'son of the servant of the bishop.'

An early record of the name dates back to 1175, when a Ewan Gillespie was witness to a charter by the Earls of Lennox, whose clan held territories in the Lowlands.

But it is with the Highland clans of Chattan and Macpherson that the Gillespies are particularly associated.

Unique in that it is actually a confederation of clans, theories of Clan Chattan's origins are that 'Chattan' derives from 'Catav', in Sutherland, that it derives from the ancient Gaulish tribe the 'Catti' or, more plausibly, that it traces back to St Cathan, the sixth century Irish monk who brought the Christian message to the Hebrides and to the Isle of Bute, on the western seaboard.

Widely revered, and with his feast day May 7,

his name survives on the landscape through a number of ruined churches and other holy sites and place names that include Kilchattan Bay and Ardchattan, on Bute.

The progenitor, or founder, of Clan Chattan is reputed to have been Gillichattan Mor, 'the great servant of St Cathan', who was baillie of the abbey lands of Ardchattan.

During the reign from 1005 to 1034 of King Malcolm II, the clan came to possess the lands of Glenloy and Loch Arkaig, in Lochaber, with the stronghold of Tor Castle the seat of the chief.

The clan's history from this point remains obscure until 1291 when Eva, a daughter of Dougal Dall, or Gilpatrick, 6th chief of the clan, married Angus Mackintosh, 6th Chief of Clan Mackintosh and who subsequently became 7th Chief of Clan Chattan.

Having established themselves at Tor Castle, the Chattans later withdrew to Rothiemurchus, near Aviemore.

Taking advantage of this, Clan Cameron occupied the Glenloy lands and thereby sparked off a bitter feud between the Chattans and Clan Cameron that lasted for centuries.

Clan Chattan, meanwhile, had evolved into

the mighty union, or confederation, of clans known collectively as Clan Chattan.

Composed of original descendants of both Clan Chattan and Clan Mackintosh and their respective cadet branches and septs, or sub-branches, this 'core' group of twelve who made up the confederation are:

Clan Davidson, Clan Farquharson, Clan MacBean, Clan MacGillivray, the Macintyres on Badenoch, Clan Mackintosh, Maclean of Dochgarroch, Clan MacPhail, Clan Macpherson, Clan Macqueen of Strathdearn, Clan MacThomas and Clan Shaw of Tordarroch.

It is through Clan Macpherson that the Gillespies – as a sept, or sub-branch of the clan – are also recognised as part of Clan Chattan and, accordingly, entitled to share in their heritage and traditions.

These include the Clan Macpherson/Clan Chattan crest of a wildcat, and motto 'Touch not the cat bot a glove.

The 'glove' referred to is the pad of the cat and 'bot' means 'without'.

When the pad is 'ungloved', this means the cat's claws are unsheathed, so the motto therefore serves as a metaphorical warning to others not to risk incurring the wrath of the Macphersons or any other members of the Clan Chattan Confederation.

Deriving their name from the Gaelic Mac a' Phearsain, denoting 'son of the parson', the Macphersons are said to descend from a Muireach, or Murdo, who was a priest at Kingussie, in Strathspey.

This was at a time when priests of the Celtic Church were allowed to marry and it was one of his descendants who, in about the late ninth century resettled in Lochaber from Badenoch.

But in 1309, according to clan tradition, the great warrior king Robert the Bruce, destined to be the victor of the battle of Bannockburn in 1314, offered the Badenoch lands to the Macphersons and their kinsfolk such as the Gillespies if they would help him destroy his enemies, the Comyns – which they duly did.

Returning to the feud between Clan Chattan and the Camerons, in 1370 the two clans and their allies met in battle at Invernahavon, southwest of Newtonmore, Strathspey.

Traditionally, the honoured position to fight in battle was on the right-wing of an army, and the Macphersons and their allies Clan Davidson hotly disputed to whom the honour should fall.

The Davidsons proved triumphant and, stung

by this, the Macphersons stomped off in high dudgeon.

But they were eventually prevailed upon to return and helped to inflict a decisive defeat on the Camerons.

In 1396, a Clan Chattan contingent fought in the famous Battle of the Clans, also known as the battle of the North Inch that took place on a large, flat meadow of the name on the outskirts of Perth.

A bitter feud had dragged out for some time between Clan Chattan and Clan Kay, a bloody vendetta that had not only visited mayhem on the clans themselves, but also periodically devastated the lives of their more peaceful neighbours.

In a desperate bid to resolve the matter, King Robert III arranged for a gladiatorial combat between the two warring factions, watched by not only the king himself but a glittering array of courtiers and even the Dauphin of France.

Sixty champions were chosen from each side, with the ferocious Shaw Macghillechrist Mhic Iain, more commonly known in Gaelic as *Sgorfhiaclach* – 'Bucktooth' - commanding the Chattan clansmen.

Armed with a deadly arsenal of swords, dirks

and axes and allowed to shoot off one volley of crossbow bolts, the 120 warriors battled it out until only eleven Chattan men were left standing on the blood-soaked field of combat.

The sole Kay survivor took to his heels and swam for safety across the River Tay.

Nearly 350 years later, as kinsfolk of the Macphersons/Clan Chattan, bearers of the Gillespie name fought for the cause of the ill-fated Charles Edward Stuart, better known to posterity as Bonnie Prince Charlie, whose hopes for the restoration of the Royal House of Stuart were crushed forever in the carnage of the battle of Culloden, fought on April 16, 1746, on the outskirts of Inverness.

Euan Macpherson of Cluny had raised a regiment of 350 men in Badenoch and played a leading role in the victory over the Hanoverian army at the battle of Falkirk on January 17.

Making their exhausted way to Culloden after engaging in a number of skirmishes to join the main Jacobite army they were met en route by survivors escaping the battlefield and Cluny Macpherson was forced to flee in order to evade capture.

With a price on his head, but loyally protected

by his kinsfolk, he led a fugitive existence for nine years before escaping to France, where he died in 1764.

Now the site of a private mansion built in the nineteenth century, Cluny Castle, about five miles south-west of Newtonmore, and one of the Macpherson strongholds, was razed to the ground by the Hanoverians in reprisal for Cluny Macpherson's active support of the Jacobite cause.

Other strongholds and properties held by the clan over the centuries include Invereshie House, near Kingussie, held by them from the fourteenth century and Pitmain House, also near Kingussie and which now forms part of the Highland Folk Museum.

A Clan Chattan Band of Union was subscribed to by all the clans that formed the confederation in 1609, and in August of 2009, to mark its 400th anniversary, all the chiefs of the Clan Chattan clans and some of their members met in Inverness to sign a new bond to renew their centuries-old kinship.

A Clan Chattan Association, meanwhile, was founded in 1933 and thrives to this day – organising a number of events in early August every year, in collaboration with Highland Sports Fair, at Moy Hall, south of Inverness, and home to the Clan Mackintosh chiefs.

Chapter three:

Crown and Covenant

In keeping with the ecclesiastical roots of their name, a number of Gillespies were actively involved in the religious affairs of their time – some paying a heavy price in the process.

During the turbulent seventeenth century, George Gillespie was the influential theologian born in 1613 in Kirkcaldy, Fife.

Graduating from St Andrews University and ordained a minister at Wemyss in 1638, and having served as chaplain to John, Viscount Kenmure and John, Earl of Cassilis, he became minister of Greyfriars Kirk, Edinburgh in 1642.

A year later, he was selected as the youngest member of the Westminster Assembly of Divines that was charged with overseeing the preparation of the *Directory and Confession of Faith*.

Adopted minister of St Giles, Edinburgh in 1647 and Moderator of the General Assembly of the Church of Scotland, he died the following year.

While he had never rebelled against the authorities, this was far from the case with his son

Robert Gillespie, born in 1643 and who became embroiled as a Covenanter in the struggles between Crown and Covenant.

Known as the War of the Three Kingdoms of Scotland, England and Ireland, and of which the English Civil War formed a part, they were sparked off in Scotland during the Bishops' Wars of 1639 and 1640.

These wars had their origin in the widely unpopular attempt by King Charles I to impose uniform religious practice between the Church of England and the proudly independent Scottish Kirk, through the introduction of the *Episcopal Book of Common Prayer*.

This acted as a catalyst for the signing on February 28, 1638 of the National Covenant – a document as important to Scottish history as the equally famed Declaration of Arbroath of 1320.

Described as 'the glorious marriage day of the kingdom with God', the Covenant renounced Roman Catholic belief, pledged to uphold the Presbyterian religion and called for free parliaments and assemblies.

First signed at Greyfriars Kirk by nobles, barons, burgesses and ministers, it was subscribed to the following day by hundreds of common folk.

Copies were made and dispatched around the nation and subscribed to by thousands more – with its adherents becoming known as Covenanters.

This led to a civil war that raged between Covenanters and Royalists in Scotland from 1638 until 1649, when Charles I was beheaded on the orders of the English Parliament – whose military arm was the New Model Army under Oliver Cromwell.

Following the restoration to the throne of Charles II in 1660, the death knell for the Covenanting movement was sounded when a Recissory Act was passed, declaring the Covenant illegal.

Episcopal rule was foisted on the Scottish Kirk, and all ministers who refused to adhere to this new order were deprived of their parishes.

Along with their congregations, many ministers literally took to the hills, preaching at open-air meetings known as conventicles.

Look-outs were posted to keep a wary eye out for the approach of Government troops, known as dragoons, and justice was literally executed on the spot for those unfortunate enough to fall into their hands.

Constantly persecuted by the forces of authority, the Covenanters rose in futile rebellion in

November of 1666 and, as a sign of the harsh treatment that was to be subsequently meted out to them, many of the prisoners taken were tortured and hanged.

A Covenanting victory was achieved at the battle of Drumclog in June of 1679, only to be followed a few short weeks later by resounding defeat at the battle of Bothwell Brig, near Hamilton, by a force commanded by the Duke of Monmouth – with nearly 800 mown down and 1,400 taken prisoner.

In a bid to stamp out the Covenanting movement, the authorities had ruled that ministers had to be 'licensed' by them, and Gillespie, as an 'unlicensed' minister who preached at conventicles and in private homes, was denounced as a rebel by the Privy Council in 1672.

Captured at a conventicle at Falkirk later that year, he was imprisoned in the near-impregnable fortress of the Bass Rock, in the Forth – the first Presbyterian minister to be incarcerated there for his beliefs.

His health broke down after enduring two months of solitary confinement in a dark and damp cell, and he was released by the Privy Council.

But in June of 1673 his name appeared on a

list of a number of ministers who were to be apprehended on sight, with a hefty reward on his head – an indication of how dangerous the authorities viewed him.

The council also did not seem to be concerned if the rebel ministers were taken dead or alive, their orders stating that anyone who 'apprehended' them would be indemnified 'for any slaughter that should be committed in apprehending them.'

Managing to evade capture, chilling notices were issued by the Privy Council in August of 1675 against Gillespie and others that prohibited anyone 'to reset, supply, or inter-commune with any of the aforesaid persons or rebels, for the causes foresaid, nor furnish them with meat, drink, house, harbour, victual, nor any other thing useful or comfortable to them …'

With these draconian restrictions in place and with the net growing tighter around him, Gillespie's subsequent fate remains obscure – with some sources asserting he fled to England and others to Holland, where he died at an unknown date.

Engaged in much more peaceful endeavours, James Gillespie was the wealthy Edinburgh snuff and tobacco merchant and snuff mill owner born in 1726 in Roslin, Midlothian.

Known for his remarkable thrift, although his employees were well-treated, he is reputed to have coined the phrase 'waste not, want not.'

He died in 1797, while his legacy survives to this day in the form of James Gillespie's High School, and also the adjoining James Gillespie's Primary School, in the Marchmont area of Edinburgh.

Established through a generous bequest from Gillespie to originally cater for the educational needs of boys from poor backgrounds, and having undergone a number of changes in ownership over the years, it also opened its doors to girls in 1923.

Across the Atlantic, Colonel John Hamilton Gillespie was the enterprising Scottish-American soldier, politician, businessman and land developer who has the distinction of creating the first golf course in Florida and the second in the United States.

Born in Edinburgh in 1852 and educated at St Andrews University, he served as a captain in the Midlothian Coast Artillery Volunteers and, after returning from military service in what was then the British colony of Australia, he left Scottish shores for the USA in 1886 to oversee his father's business, the Florida Mortgage and Investment Company, based in Sarasota.

Overhauling the business and resolving to settle in Sarasota, he transformed it into a thriving community and, as a keen golfer – having learned to play the game while a student at St Andrews, the home of golf – he laid out two golf courses on his property.

These were the first in Florida and the second in the United States, while in 1905 he built a nine-hole course on the site of what is now the Sarasota County Courthouse, while also laying out courses in Tampa, Florida and even the Cuban capital, Havana.

Sarasota, meanwhile, was incorporated as a town in 1902, and Gillespie elected its first mayor.

Also instrumental in the founding of the Episcopal Church in Sarasota – the Church of the Redeemer – he was ordained as a deacon before his death in 1923.

Chapter four:

On the world stage

Bearers of the Gillespie name have gained international acclaim and established enduring legacies through a colourful range of endeavours and pursuits.

A pioneer in the development of modern jazz and the 'bebop' genre, John Birks Gillespie was the American trumpeter, bandleader, singer and composer better known to his legions of fans as **Dizzy Gillespie**.

Born into a musical family in Cheraw, South Carolina in 1917, his father was a local bandleader, while the young protégé began to play the piano when he was aged only five and, by the time he was aged twelve, had learned to play both the trumpet and trombone.

Attending the Laurinburg Institute in North Carolina for two years, he moved to Philadelphia when he was aged 18 and secured his first professional job as a musician with the Frank Fairfax Orchestra.

His nickname 'Dizzy' proved apt as he subsequently progressed through playing for a dizzying number of bands including, in 1939, Cab

Calloway's Orchestra and, a year later, recording along with the orchestra his composition *Pickin' the Cabbage*.

With his trade-mark horn-rimmed spectacles, beret, 'scat' style of singing and familiar banter with the audience, he became an extremely popular figure among jazz aficionados while also writing band music for both Jimmy Dorsey and Woody Herman.

Flitting from band to band, including Ella Fitzgerald's orchestra, it was along with saxophonist Charlie Parker that he developed the bebop style – forming along with Parker in 1945 Dizzy Gillespie and the Bebop Six, featured in the film of that year *Jivin' in Be-Bop*.

With his tongue firmly in cheek, he stood as an independent candidate during the 1964 U.S. Presidential Campaign, vowing that if elected he would rename the White House the Blues House and form a cabinet of fellow jazz luminaries such as Duke Ellington as Secretary of State, Miles Davis as Director of the CIA and Charlie Mingus as 'Secretary of Peace.'

Having influenced generations of musicians, he died in 1993 and is the recipient of a host of honours and awards.

These include a Grammy Lifetime Achievement Award and the American Society of Composers, Authors and Publishers' Duke Ellington Award 'for his achievement as a composer, performer and bandleader.'

In America's legendary Tin Pan Alley of songwriters, James Lamont Gillespie was the composer better known by his pen name **Haven Gillespie**.

Born into a poor family in Covington, Kentucky in 1888, he worked as a newspaper typesetter, supplementing his income by playing and singing songs he had written at local vaudeville shows.

By 1911, in collaboration with other writers, he began writing songs for which at the outset he received only meagre royalties through the sales of sheet music.

But he progressed to greater fortune by co-composing a number of popular songs including *Breezin' Along With The Breeze*, *You Go to My Head*, *Honey*, *Beautiful Love* and, from 1934, the enduring Christmas favourite *Santa Claus is Comin' to Town*.

He died in 1975, three years after his induction into the Songwriters Hall of Fame.

In contemporary times, **Bobby Gillespie** is the Scottish musician and singer-songwriter known as the former drummer of the band The Jesus and Mary Chain and founding member of alternative rock band Primal Scream.

Born in the Mount Florida area of Glasgow in 1962, his father is the former Scottish trades union official Bob Gillespie.

Having toured with bands and artists including Jethro Tull, Meat Loaf and Chris De Burgh, **Mark Gillespie** is the singer-songwriter born in Stockport, Greater Manchester, in 1970.

Touring with his Mark Gillespie Band and with albums that include the 2009 *In Your Hands*, in 2011 he also co-founded the Pink Floyd tribute band Kings of Floyd.

With the rather impressive birth-name Richenda Antionette de Winterstein Gillespie, **Dana Gillespie** is the English singer, songwriter and actress whose first single was the 1965 *Thank You Boy*.

Born in Woking, Surrey in 1949 and having recorded a number of albums, she is also known as the original Mary Magdalene in the first London production, in 1972, of the musical *Jesus Christ Superstar*.

Her first claim to fame, however, dates back to 1962 – when she was British Junior Water Skiing Champion.

Back across the Atlantic, **Darlene Gillespie**, born in Montreal in 1941, is the Canadian-American former child actress best known as a singer and dancer from 1955 to 1959 on the *Mickey Mouse Club* television show – quitting the world of show business for a career in nursing when the series ended.

In the highly competitive world of sport, **Gary Gillespie** is the Scottish former football defender, born in Stirling in 1960, who played for teams including Falkirk, Coventry City, Liverpool and Celtic and the recipient of 33 caps playing for his national team.

Earning 86 caps playing for his national team, **Keith Gillespie**, born in Larne in 1975, is the Northern Irish former football winger who played for a number of teams including Manchester United, Newcastle United and Sheffield United.

From football to baseball, **Brock Gillespie**, born in 1982 in Des Moines, Iowa is the American professional player who has played for Spanish team CB Ciudad Valladolid, having previously played on home soil in the Western Athletic Conference for Rice

University – while on screen he appears in the 2006 baseball-themed film *Glory Road*.

On the cricket pitch **John Gillespie**, born in Sydney in 1975, is the Australian cricket coach and former fast bowler and low-order batsman who played at first-class level for South Australia, Glamorgan and Yorkshire.

From sport to the media, **Bill Gillespie** is the globe-trotting Canadian journalist, author and foreign correspondent born in 1946 in Melfort, Saskatchewan.

World hot-spots he has covered include Afghanistan, Chechnya and Iraq – where on April 9, 2003 he witnessed the toppling of Saddam Hussein's statue in Baghdad's central square.

Bearers of the Gillespie name have also excelled in the highly creative world of art.

Born in 1876 in Bonnybridge, Stirlingshire, **Janetta Gillespie** was the Scottish artist and graduate of Glasgow School of Art known for her use of the chiaroscuro technique in her paintings mainly of flowers and still life compositions.

Having exhibited widely and winner of the Glasgow Society of Women Artists Lauder Award in 1934, she died in 1956, while her brother Alexander and younger sister Floris were also accomplished artists.

Born in 1882, **Floris Gillespie**, in common with her sister, also studied at Glasgow School of Art and was also a winner, in 1948, of the Lauder Award; she died in 1967.

From art to the silver screen, **William Gillespie** was the Scottish actor who played in about 180 films between 1915 and 1939.

Born in Aberdeen in 1894 and immigrating to the United States, he appeared in films mainly during Hollywood's silent era, supporting comedians including Laurel and Hardy and Charlie Chaplin and normally in the role of an obstructive official.

Having also supported Harold Lloyd in films that include the 1917 *The Cure* and, from 1922, *A Quiet Street*, he died in 1938.

In contemporary times, **Robert Gillespie**, born in Lille, France, in 1933, is the British actor, director and writer whose screen credits include the 1976 *At the Earth's Core*, the 1978 *Force 10 from Navarone*, the 1980 *Keep It in the Family* and, from 2018, *Peterloo*.

Behind the camera lens, Arnold Gillespie, better known as **Buddy Gillespie**, was the award-winning special effects artist born in 1899 in El Paso, Texas.

Joining MGM in 1925 and appointed head of its special effects department in 1936, before his death in 1978 he was the recipient of Academy Awards for special effects and photography for the 1939 *The Wizard of Oz,* the 1942 *Mrs Miniver*, the 1959 *Ben Hur* and, from 1962, *Mutiny on the Bounty*.

Also behind the camera lens, **Craig Gillespie** is the award-winning Australian film, television and commercial director, born in Sydney in 1967, whose credits include the 2007 *Mr Woodstock*, the 2011 *Fright Night* and 2017's *Tonya*.

One bearer of the Gillespie name who bequeathed a particularly popular legacy for animal lovers was **Thomas Haining Gillespie**, the founder of Edinburgh Zoo.

Born in Dumfries, in the southwest of Scotland, in 1876, he qualified as a solicitor – but his passion was zoology.

Thomas resolved to overcome the obstacles posed by Scotland's climate to exotic species by establishing a zoological park.

With the help of Edinburgh City Council, this came to fruition in 1913 when the Scottish Zoological Park – better known today to its thousands of annual visitors as Edinburgh Zoo – was opened.

Serving as the zoo's director from 1913 until 1950, and having in 1909 founded the Royal Zoological Society of Scotland, he also furthered interest in the subject among children through hosting a BBC Scottish Children's Hour radio programme as 'The Zoo Man', talking about the animals in the zoo and answering questions submitted by his young listeners.

The series proved so popular that, from 1930 until it ended in the late 1950s, it was also broadcast throughout the rest of the United Kingdom, and *Zoo Tales* books based on the programmes proved best-sellers.

Also elected a Fellow of the Royal Society of Edinburgh, he died in 1967.